RABBITS

by Sophie Geister-Jones

Cody Koala
An Imprint of Pop!
popbooksonline.com

abdobooks.com

Published by Pop!, a division of ABDO, PO Box 398166, Minneapolis, Minnesota 55439. Copyright © 2020 by POP, LLC. International copyrights reserved in all countries. No part of this book may be reproduced in any form without written permission from the publisher. Pop!™ is a trademark and logo of POP, LLC.

Printed in the United States of America, North Mankato, Minnesota

102019
012020

THIS BOOK CONTAINS
RECYCLED MATERIALS

Cover Photo: Blue Jean Images/Alamy
Interior Photos: Blue Jean Images/Alamy, 1; iStockphoto, 5 (top), 5 (bottom left), 7, 11, 13 (top), 13 (bottom left), 13 (bottom right), 14, 15, 18, 21; FLPA/Alamy, 8; Shutterstock Images, 17

Editor: Meg Gaertner
Series Designer: Sophie Geister-Jones

Library of Congress Control Number: 2019942774

Publisher's Cataloging-in-Publication Data

Names: Geister-Jones, Sophie, author

Title: Rabbits / by Sophie Geister-Jones

Description: Minneapolis, Minnesota : Pop!, 2020 | Series: Pets | Includes online resources and index.

Identifiers: ISBN 9781532165726 (lib. bdg.) | ISBN 9781532167041 (ebook)

Subjects: LCSH: Rabbits--Juvenile literature. | Rabbits as pets--Juvenile literature. | Pets--Juvenile literature. | Rabbits--Behavior--Juvenile literature.

Classification: DDC 636.932--dc23

Hello! My name is

Cody Koala

Pop open this book and you'll find QR codes like this one, loaded with information, so you can learn even more!

Scan this code* and others like it while you read, or visit the website below to make this book pop.

popbooksonline.com/rabbits

*Scanning QR codes requires a web-enabled smart device with a QR code reader app and a camera.

Table of Contents

Chapter 1

Behavior

Rabbits are smart and quiet animals. They sleep during the day and night. They are awake in the early morning and in the evening.

Watch a video here!

Rabbits are active when they are awake. They play with toys. They play with one another. Rabbits explore their surroundings. They hop around.

thumping

Sometimes rabbits thump. They hit the ground with their back feet. Rabbits thump when they sense danger. Rabbits might also **binky**. They jump and twist their bodies. Rabbits binky when they are happy.

History

Humans have been keeping rabbits for **centuries**. At first, people raised rabbits for food. But in the 1700s, they started keeping rabbits as **companions**.

Learn more here!

Many Types of Rabbits

There are more than 40 **breeds** of pet rabbits. Each breed looks different. Rabbits can be many sizes and colors. Their fur can be short or long.

Learn more here!

For example, some rabbits
are big. Their ears stand up.
They are fluffy.

Other rabbits are small.

Their ears are floppy. They

have spots.

Chapter 4

Rabbit Care

Pet rabbits live in cages. Cages should be cleaned regularly. And they should be indoors. That way, rabbits are safe from wild animals.

Complete an activity here!

Rabbits need daily **exercise**. Owners should let their rabbits explore outside of their cages. Rabbits can explore a person's home. Or they can explore a fenced area outside.

Owners should always watch their rabbits when they are exploring. This way rabbits won't chew on things they aren't supposed to. And they won't dig under fences.

Rabbits drink water. They eat hay, leafy greens, and food pellets. They chew on toys. Owners can talk to a **vet** about their rabbits' needs.

A rabbit's top front teeth never stop growing. Chewing helps keep these teeth short.

leafy greens

Making Connections

Text-to-Self

Do you know someone who has a pet rabbit? What color is the rabbit? How does it play?

Text-to-Text

Have you read other books about rabbits? What did you learn?

Text-to-World

Why would it be important for rabbit owners to know the difference between thumping and binkying?

Glossary

binky – to jump up and twist around because of happiness and comfort.

breed – a group of animals that all look similar.

century – a period of 100 years.

companion – a person or animal that is friendly and spends time with another person or animal.

exercise – activity that requires physical movement and improves health.

vet – a doctor who takes care of animals.

Index

Online Resources

popbooksonline.com

Thanks for reading this Cody Koala book!

Scan this code* and others like it in this book, or visit the website below to make this book pop!

popbooksonline.com/rabbits

*Scanning QR codes requires a web-enabled smart device with a QR code reader app and a camera.